**Learner Services**

Please return
on or before
the last date
stamped below

CITY COLLEGE
**NORWICH**

Andy Croft

Published in association with The Basic Skills Agency

# Hodder Murray

A MEMBER OF THE HODDER HEADLINE GROUP

The Publishers would like to thank the following for permission to reproduce copyright material:

Hodder Headline and Jonny Wilkinson for the quotes on pages 22 and 23 from *My World* by Jonny Wilkinson.

**Photo credits**
p.iv © Chris Barry/Rex features; pp.5, 8, 15, 21, 26 © David Rogers/Getty Images; p.11 © Odd Andersen/Getty Images.


Orders: please contact Bookpoint Ltd, 130 Milton Park, Abingdon, Oxon OX14 4SB. Telephone: (44) 01235 827720. Fax: (44) 01235 400454. Lines are open from 9.00–6.00, Monday to Saturday, with a 24-hour message answering service. Visit our website at www.hoddereducation.co.uk.


© Andy Croft 2005
First published in 2005 by
Hodder Murray, a member of the Hodder Headline Group
338 Euston Road
London NW1 3BH

Impression number    10 9 8 7 6 5 4 3 2
Year                            2010  2009  2008  2007  2006

Cover photo © Greg Wood/AFP/Getty Images
Typeset in 14pt Palatino by SX Composing DTP, Rayleigh, Essex.
Printed in Great Britain by CPI Bath.

A catalogue record for this title is available from the British Library

ISBN-10 0 340 90063 6
ISBN-13 978 0 340 90063 5

# Contents

Jonny Wilkinson.

# 1 Jonny

He is strong.
He is fast.
He is brave.
He can run.
He can tackle.
He has good hands.
He can kick with both feet.

He is a World Cup winner.
He is the best fly-half in the world.

He is Jonny Wilkinson.

# 2 Beginnings

Jonny Peter Wilkinson was born on 25 May 1979
in Frimley, Surrey.
His dad, Phil, used to play rugby and cricket.
His mum, Philippa, played squash at county level.

Jonny started playing mixed rugby
(for boys and girls)
when he was four years old.

He went to school at Lord Wandsworth College
near Basingstoke.
He played rugby for the school team.
He also played for Farnham Juniors.

Jonny worked hard at school.

He worked even harder at rugby.

He used to practise kicking every dinner-time.

He practised after school,

at weekends

and in the holidays.

He wanted to be good.

He wanted to be the best.

Sometimes his parents had to stop him practising!

Jonny also played tennis and basketball.

He played cricket and rugby for Hampshire schools.

He played football for Farnham Town.

But rugby was always his favourite game.

The scoring in rugby is a bit complicated.
If you touch the ball down behind the line
you get five points (a try).
If you kick a dead ball between the posts
and over the bar you get two points (a conversion)
or three points (a penalty).
If you bounce the ball on the ground
and then kick it between the posts
you get three points (a drop goal).
Not many rugby players can do all these things.
Jonny can.

When he was aged 15,
Jonny played for England under-16s.
In 1997 he went to Australia
with an English Schools' team.
He scored 94 points in only five games!
He scored 38 points for England under-18s.
They won the junior Grand Slam.
He played for England under-21s.
He scored 11 points in one game against France.

Jonny when he played for England under-21s.

# 3 Newcastle Falcons

Jonny took three A Levels in
Biology, Chemistry and French.
He was planning to go to Durham University.
But then his old games teacher, Steve Bates,
went to coach Newcastle Falcons.
He asked Jonny to go with him.

Jonny decided not to go to university.
Instead he signed for Newcastle Falcons.
They are a very old rugby club.
They play at Kingston Park in Newcastle.

In his first season,
Jonny came on as a substitute
in several games.
But he was only in the starting line-up
for one game.
He played centre against Exeter.
He scored a conversion and a penalty.

The next year he played 13 league games.
He scored three tries, 39 penalties,
11 conversions and three drop goals.
Jonny Wilkinson had arrived.
In March 1998, Jonny was named
Rugby World Player of the Month.

Over the next three seasons
he scored 618 points in 48 league games.
That's nearly 13 points in every game.
That's amazing.

In 1999, Jonny and the Newcastle Falcons
lost the Tetley Bitter Cup Final.
But they were back two years later – and won it.

In 2002, Jonny was named
International Player of the Year.
He was made Falcons' team captain.

By the start of 2004–5
Jonny had scored 1158 points for Falcons.
He is their record scorer.
He holds the records for the most penalties scored
and for the most drop goals.

Jonny playing for Newcastle Falcons.

# 4 Six Nations

Every year England, Scotland, Wales, Ireland,
France and Italy play each other at rugby.
This is called the Six Nations.

In 1998, Jonny was included in the England squad
to play against Scotland.
He was only 18.
But he was ready for England.

The next year he was in the starting line-up
against Scotland.
He played centre.
He kicked four goals.
England won.
He scored seven penalties against Ireland.

In 2000, Jonny scored all 15 points against France.
England won the Six Nations that year.

In 2001, he scored his first try for England.
He also scored six conversions and
five penalties in the same game.
England won the Six Nations again.

In 2002, he scored 30 points against Wales.
After this English rugby fans voted Jonny
the greatest fly-half of all time.

In 2003, he scored 77 points in the Six Nations.
England won the Grand Slam.

Jonny and the England Rugby team after wining the Grand Slam in 2003.

# 5 Wilko

What makes Jonny Wilkinson
the best fly-half in the world?

Jonny is only 5′ 10″ (1.79 m) tall.
But he weighs 13st 7lbs (85.7 kg).
He is strong.
He is brave.

Not every fly-half likes tackling.
But Jonny does.
He has good hands.
And two good feet.

He practises all the time.
He is always first on the training ground.
And the last to leave.
He trains for eight hours a day.
He trains on his days off.
He even trains on Christmas Day.

He practises kicking the ball for hours.
He tries to hit the cross-bar.
He pretends there is a woman called 'Doris'
sitting behind the posts.
He tries to hit her with the ball!
Jonny's training always ends with six kicks.
They must all be perfect or he has to start again.
This once took five hours!

Jonny's training includes boxing and football.
He has three coaches:
Dave Reddin, Dave Aldred and Steve Black.

Jonny eats lots of chicken and pastrami.
He never eats crisps, chocolate or junk food.
He doesn't drink. He doesn't smoke.
He hates smoking.

When he takes a penalty
he always holds his hands together first.
It looks like he is praying,
but he is trying to block out all the noise.
He taps his left toe on the grass.
He tries to focus on the ball.
Then he shoots – and scores!

# 6 Down Under

In 1998, Jonny was picked
for the England tour of Australia.
Most of the senior players couldn't go.
So young players like Jonny
were given their chance.

It was a disaster.
Everything went wrong.
The young England team
was no match for the Aussies.
Australia won 76–0.
England lost all seven matches.
It was the 'Tour from Hell'.
But Jonny says he learned a lot.
'It taught me more than anything else,' he says.

Jonny playing for England against Australia in 2002.

Jonny went back to Australia
three summers later
with the British Lions.

In November 2002, Jonny led England
to victory over New Zealand.
He scored 21 points in a 31–28 thriller.
A week later, England beat Australia 32–31.
Jonny scored 22 points.
Revenge!
England was the best side in world rugby.

Jonny is England's all-time highest scorer.
He has scored twice as many points
as any other England rugby player.

# 7 The Rugby World Cup

In the 1999 World Cup,
Jonny scored over 100 points
in friendly games against the USA and Canada.

He scored against New Zealand, Fiji
and South Africa.
But he was dropped for the quarter-finals.
Without Jonny, England was knocked out.

The next World Cup was played
in Australia in 2003.
Clive Woodward was the England coach.
Martin Johnson was the England captain.
The team included some great players:
Mike Catt, Jason Robinson, Ben Cohen,
Matt Dawson, Richard Hill, Lawrence Dallaglio –
and Jonny Wilkinson.

England beat Georgia 84–6.
Jonny scored two penalties.

England beat South Africa 25–6.
Jonny scored one conversion, four penalties and
one drop goal.

England beat Samoa 35–22.
Jonny scored three conversions, two penalties and
one drop goal.

In the quarter-finals England beat Wales 28–17.
Jonny scored one conversion, six penalties and
one drop goal.

In the semi-final England beat France 24–7.
Jonny scored all England's points
with five penalties and three drop goals.

England was in the final of the Rugby World Cup.
But they had to play Australia.
The old enemy.

It was a difficult  game.
Both sides tried their best.
It was raining hard.
Australia took the lead, but Jonny kicked
three penalties.
He set up Jason Robinson for a try.
At half-time England was leading 14–5.
Could they hang on?

In the second half
Australia equalised with three penalties.
The game went into extra time.
Jonny scored another penalty.
But Australia drew level again.
Both teams were tired.

Then, with only 26 seconds left
Matt Dawson passed the ball back.
Jonny caught it in front of the posts.
He looked up.
The Australians ran towards him
to block the kick.
Jonny drop-kicked it.
It was a perfect shot.
The ball flew straight between the posts.
20–17 to England!

England and Jonny Wilkinson
had won the Rugby World Cup!

Jonny's winning drop-kick goal against Australia in 2003.

# 8 Jonny Says

'Preparation is power.'

'If I train harder and better than anyone else,
I will come out on top.'

'I only get the points because
I have team-mates who do the work.'

'I play with a fear of letting people down.'

'I never asked to be famous.
I just wanted to play rugby.'

'If I can smile when I'm out there
I believe I can unlock more
of what I have to give.'

'The harder I work the more likely I am to succeed.'

'If I tell myself I'm doing well,
it will help me to do so.'

'I know I'm only part of the way to
becoming the player I want to be.'

'I train to the point where my shirt is drenched,
my body is screaming at me
and I feel like I'm going to be sick.'

'If you get knocked down,
make sure you get straight back up again.'

# 9 Jonny Mania

Jonny Wilkinson is a World Cup winner.
He is captain of Newcastle Falcons.
He is England captain.

Jonny is sometimes called
the David Beckham of rugby.
Jonny and Beckham are friends.

After the World Cup in 2003
Jonny was voted BBC Sports Personality
of the Year.
He was voted the Most Fanciable Man in Britain.
He won the Haircut of the Year award.
He was given an MBE by the Queen in 2003.
The next year he was given an OBE.
There is even a wax model of Jonny
in Madame Tussaud's in London.

Jonny helps raise money for charity,
especially for the NSPCC.

But Jonny hates being famous.
He is a shy and private man.
He doesn't want to be a 'celebrity'.
He just wants to play rugby.
He turns down lots of adverts,
especially for junk food.
A magazine wanted photos
of the inside of Jonny's house.
They offered him £1 million.
But Jonny said no.

He still sees a lot of his mum and dad.
They are a very close family.
His favourite food is his mum's banana loaf.
He lives with his brother Mark
in a quiet Northumbrian village.
Mark also plays for Newcastle Falcons.

Jonny wants to have a big family one day.
His girlfriend Diana
is an actress, model and TV presenter.
They met when she was a student in Newcastle.
She was working as a barmaid.
Jonny and Diana like running together
and playing golf.

Jonny and his girlfriend, Diana, when he was awarded his MBE in 2003.

Jonny supports Newcastle United.
His favourite films are *The Matrix*
and *Dumb and Dumber*.
His favourite bands are Coldplay,
The Verve, Oasis,
Travis and the Stereophonics.
Jonny is learning to play the guitar.
He wants to learn to play the piano.
He is learning to speak French and Spanish.

After the 2003 World Cup
Jonny was injured.
He had to have an operation.
He was out of action for eight months.
Now he is back –
better and stronger than ever.
Australia – watch out!

# 10 Jonny Quiz

1   When is Jonny's birthday?

2   What club does he play for?

3   How many points do you score for a drop goal?

4   How old was Jonny when he won
his first full England cap?

5   What is the name of the invisible woman
behind the goal?

6   Who was England captain in the 2003 Rugby
World Cup final?

7   How many points did Jonny score in the 2003
Rugby World Cup final?

8   How many times has Jonny played
for the British Lions?

9   What football team does Jonny support?

10  Does Jonny like being famous?